THE BLUEPRINT

THE YOUNG MAN'S GUIDE TO BECOMING AN EXCELLENT HUSBAND

Written By

James Bass

CLARICE JEFFERIES

The Blueprint

The Young Man's Guide to Becoming

An Excellent Husband

by James Bass

Published by Clarice Jefferies Publishing

Contact info: cjpublishing@yahoo.com

Copyright © 2023 James Bass

All rights reserved

No part of this publication may be copied, distributed, or transmitted in any form or by any means, including photocopying, recording, or other electronic or mechanical methods, without the prior written permission of the publisher, except in the case of brief quotations embodied in reviews and specific other non- commercial uses permitted by copyright law.

For permissions, contact:

cjpublishing@yahoo.com

Printed in the United States of America
on responsibly sourced paper

Disclaimer

I am sharing observations and information based on my experiences as a man and husband. I am not a licensed financial advisor, doctor, or mental health practitioner and I cannot provide medical advice or diagnoses. This material is solely for educational and informational purposes, and it is entirely up to you to apply it to your own life. If you require financial, medical, or mental health care, you should seek the advice of a licensed professional.

THE BLUEPRINT

TABLE OF CONTENTS

Dedication	7
Dear Son	9
To My Grandsons	11
Preface	13
Chapter 1 The Truth About Dating	17
Pysical Attraction Vs Emotional Intelligence	19
The Friend Zone	23
Be True To Yourself While Dating	27
Beware Of Manipulative Women: Mythomania & Pseudologia Fantastica	29
Mythomania	35
Pseudologia Fantastica	39
Chapter 2 Navigating Married Life	43
Home Is Where The Heart Your Wife Is	45
The Art Of Love In Marriage	49
Abandon The 50/50 Mentality	53
Your Wife Vs Your Sports	57
Emotions Are Not Only For Women	61

TABLE OF CONTENTS

    Some Practical Advice For Your Future Together Life Insurance +
Estate Planning: A Will And Trust Fund   67

    Life Insurance   69

    Estate Planning: A Will & Trust   73

Chapter 3 The Influence Of Environment   77

    The Wrong Advice From The "Right Man"   79

    From Momma's Boy To Husband Part 1   83

    From Momma's Boy To Husband Pt. 2   87

    From Momma's Boy To Husband Pt. 3   89

    Is Rap Music Influencing Your Behavior?   93

    Being "Whipped" Vs Honoring Your Wife   97

    Don't Be A Hypocrit   101

Chapter 4 How To Be A Supportive Husband In Tough Times   105

    How To Support Your Wife Through Menopause   107

    How To Support Your Wife Through Depression   113

    How To Support Your Wife Through Past Child Abuse Trauma   119

    How To Supprt Your Wife Through Past Relationship Abuse   123

    How To Support Your Wife Through Ptsd   127

Chapter 5 When To Seek Help   131

    The Benefits Of Psychological Therapy   133

Conclusions   139

    Men, Learn How To Say I Love You   141

Prayer   145

DEDICATION

DEAR SON

I cannot help but feel immense pride in the person you have become. It seems like just yesterday when I first laid eyes on you, and now you've grown up and are making a name for yourself in the world.

I want to express my pride in you. Your unwavering determination, resilience, and kindness have been a constant source of inspiration for me. Witnessing your ability to overcome challenges and achieve your goals has been remarkable, and I feel honored to call you, my son.

As you reach the age of 30, I can't help but reflect on my life at your age. You possess all the qualities I once hoped for - success, ambition, and a compassionate heart. Your ability to stay ahead of the curve is admirable, and I do not doubt that you will continue to accomplish remarkable things in the future.

THE BLUEPRINT

I want you to know that you are deeply loved and valued.

With all my love and admiration,

Your,

Dad, Father, Friend

TO MY GRANDSONS

I hope this book finds both of you in good health and high spirits. It brings me immense joy to have the opportunity to share my wisdom with both of you through this book, and I want you both to know that you hold an exceptional place in my heart.

As your grandfather, it fills my heart with pride to see the incredible individuals you are becoming. You are both blessed with unique qualities and talents, and you have the potential to achieve great things.

Life is a journey filled with ups and downs, challenges, and triumphs. Along the way, you will encounter various experiences, meet different people, and face many choices. I want you to navigate this journey with confidence, resilience, and kindness.

THE BLUEPRINT

That is why I have chosen to construct this book. Within these pages, you will find lessons learned from my own difficult experiences. I want this book to be your companion, a source of guidance, and a reminder that you are never alone.

As you delve into the pages, you will find inspiration, lessons, and solace. May it ignite your imagination, broaden your horizons, and encourage you to dream big. Remember, you have the power to shape your destiny, and this book is here to remind you of that.

But beyond the words and stories, my love for you both is immeasurable. It transcends the pages of this book and stretches across time and space.

Never doubt your worth, for you are capable of greatness. Embrace your uniqueness, follow your passions, and always treat others with kindness and respect. I am here for you both, ready to offer guidance, support, and a listening ear whenever needed.

As you go through life, always love yourself and those around you. Spread love wherever you go, as it is through love that we find purpose and fulfillment.

I am excited to see the notable accomplishments you will achieve and your positive impact on the world.

With all my love,

Your Grandfather

PREFACE

In November of 2023, my wife and I will celebrate 31 years of being together. Our marriage has been something that I have had to fight for, it has not been easy but it has been well worth the struggle. I am a man who endured relentless physical, emotional, and mental abuse from the tender age of 4 until the end of my adolescence at 17, and I know firsthand the devastating impact that child abuse can have on one's life and how it can shape and mold a man's beliefs and behaviors. I suffered this abuse at the hands of my mother and two stepfathers and the scars left by those experiences run deep, but they have also equipped me with a profound understanding of the human spirit's resilience and the power of healing.

Surviving such horrors has instilled an unyielding determination to break free from the cycle of pain and transform it into strength. Through my journey, I have gained invaluable insights into the complexities of emotional pain, the importance of emotional well-being, and the profound impact of creating a healthy marriage. This unique perspective allows me to empathize deeply with men who have endured similar traumas and guide them toward personal growth. By drawing upon my own experiences, I can help you overcome your pain and emerge as the best version of yourself, empowering you to become a loving, compassionate, and supportive husband that can build a nurturing, long lasting marriage.

"The Blueprint" takes a holistic approach to self-improvement, addressing various aspects of a man's life, including mental and emotional well-being, relationships, and personal development. By combining my personal experiences and psychological insights, I will help you understand how to be a great husband and more importantly, why.

Furthermore, "The Blueprint" offers guidance on fostering deep connections, resolving conflicts, and nurturing self-love. Understanding the delicate balance between strength and vulnerability, this book will empower you to build a solid foundation in your marriage, enhancing your overall well-being and personal growth.

I invite you to embark on this transformative journey with me. "The Blueprint" is not just a book; it is a guiding light, illuminating the path toward self-discovery, and self-mastery. Together, we can overcome the challenges that have held us back and unlock the immense potential that lies within each one of us.

Remember, you are not alone in this process. I have been where you are, and I believe that every man has the strength to rise above his circumstances and create a life of purpose and fulfillment. Let us embark on this extraordinary journey together, embracing the power of "The Blueprint" to shape our lives and become the best husbands we can be.

Chapter 1
THE TRUTH ABOUT DATING

PYSICAL ATTRACTION VS EMOTIONAL INTELLIGENCE

We are all wired to be physically attracted to others, and it's an instinct that drives us toward potential mates and aids us in finding reproductive partners. Physical attraction alone isn't enough to keep a long-term relationship, but it can be a key factor in keeping you from leaving.

For men, physical attraction is often more important in romantic relationships. Men are more visually stimulated than women and are more likely to pursue someone based on their physical appearance. While this may appear superficial to some, it is simply a fact of human nature.

Strong physical attraction to your partner can help keep you from straying. When attracted to your partner, you are less likely to be tempted by others. You'll feel fulfilled and satisfied in your relationship, making you less likely to look elsewhere for validation or intimacy.

Taking care of your physical appearance can also help you maintain the spark in your relationship. A healthy diet and regular exercise can improve physical health and attractiveness. Shaving or getting a haircut can also make you feel more confident and attractive.

It is critical to recognize that physical attraction is not the only factor contributing to a happy relationship. Other characteristics, such as shared values, trust, and communication, are also essential.

We live in a society where physical appearance is frequently prioritized when selecting a partner. However, I urge you to look deeper and consider a woman's emotional intelligence.

The ability to understand and manage one's own emotions, as well as empathize and connect with others, is referred to as emotional intelligence. A woman with high emotional intelligence will be able to communicate effectively, handle conflicts gracefully, and demonstrate empathy for you and others.

It's critical to remember that physical appearance is fleeting, and emotional intelligence is what will help a relationship last. While attraction to your partner is essential, it isn't the only factor contributing to a healthy and fulfilling relationship.

Here are some things that may help you recognize a partner with high emotional intelligence:

❖ Look for someone who can effectively communicate:

Communication is essential for a successful relationship. Find someone willing to listen and express themselves clearly.

❖ Examine how they handle difficult situations:

An emotionally intelligent woman can handle conflicts with grace and maturity.

❖ Take note of their empathy:

Is your potential partner compassionate to others? Are they able to put themselves in the shoes of others and understand their point of view?

❖ Concentrate on shared values and goals:

A woman with high emotional intelligence will share your values and goals, and this will lay the groundwork for your relationship.

Never give up. It's okay to move on if you're not feeling fulfilled or happy in your current dating situation. Don't settle for someone just because you find them attractive or believe you should be in a relationship with them because you don't want to be alone.

Knowing what you want and sticking to your guns is critical when finding a partner. Don't let peer pressure or family pressure influence your decision. You deserve to be with someone who brings you joy, so be truthful with yourself. Take the time to consider what you truly desire in a partner. Don't be afraid to express your desires and needs, even if they differ from what others have told you to look for.

Remember, physical beauty fades over time; maintaining physical attraction can effectively prevent infidelity and preserve the strength of your relationship, but emotional intelligence can last a lifetime.

THE FRIEND ZONE

I want to shed light on a topic that I've watched cause discomfort and worry in my own family- falling into the "friend zone" or the fear of becoming your wife's best friend. This generational misinformation has made some of the men in my family believe that their romantic love will fade and they will become bored if they became friends with their wives; I've witnessed the devasting impact this belief can have, watching my uncles divorce my aunts after decades of marriage. However, the reality is that embracing friendship with your wife can strengthen and deepen your relationship.

As I've gotten older, I've learned that love and friendship are not mutually exclusive, and in fact, they can coexist and complement each other in a profound way. When you become your wife's best friend, you create an unbreakable bond. She will confide in you, share her deepest secrets, and rely on your unwavering support. By fostering this trust, you establish a safe space for open communication and emotional intimacy within your marriage.

Think back to when you first laid eyes on your wife, when you were trying to date her - before romance and love blossomed, friendship played a crucial role in bringing you together; it laid the groundwork for your relationship. Remember the laughter, the shared interests, and the moments of genuine connection? These aspects create a solid foundation that can withstand the test of time. So, why not build on it?

Best friends have unparalleled understanding, and the same applies to your relationship with your wife. When you become her best friend, you take the time to honestly know her hopes, fears, joys, and frustrations. You will foster a deep understanding of how to bring out the best in her. This understanding will strengthen your bond and allow you to navigate the highlights and pitfalls of life together.

Friends share laughter and joy, and your wife deserves the same experience within your relationship. As her best friend, you can bring lightness and humor into her life, turning even the most mundane moments into cherished memories. Being her source of laughter, you'll cultivate happiness and create a positive atmosphere in your marriage.

True friends inspire each other to grow and become better individuals. By being your wife's best friend, you can encourage her personal and professional development. Support her ambitions, challenge her to reach for the stars, and be her biggest cheerleader. Together, you can create a relationship that fosters growth and empowers both of you to thrive.

Life can throw curveballs, and your wife needs someone to lean on during those challenging times. You become her pillar of strength by being her best friend, providing unwavering emotional support. Your empathy, understanding, and willingness to be there for her will show her that she's never alone in this journey.

So, let go of any reservations you may have and embrace the incredible role of being your wife's best friend. Cherish the moments of laughter, be there through thick and thin, and be the partner she can always count on and the friend she can share a lifetime of adventures with.

BE TRUE TO YOURSELF WHILE DATING

Finding a partner with whom to share your life with is an important decision for a man. However, it can be tempting to pretend to be someone you're not to impress prospective partners. While it may work in the short term, remember that a healthy and fulfilling relationship is built on honesty and authenticity.

This entails being open and honest about your values, interests, and goals. Don't try to shape yourself into the person your potential partner wants you to be. If you try to be someone you're not or suppress your genuine thoughts and feelings, you may feel disconnected from yourself and others. You may also feel anxious or depressed if you do not follow your values and needs. So instead, embrace and be proud of your unique qualities.

If you are true to yourself, you will attract a partner who values and accepts you for who you are. This lays a solid foundation for a long-lasting and healthy relationship. Remember that the goal is to find someone who completes you as well as someone who compliments you. Being honest about your flaws and weaknesses is part of being true to yourself. Nobody is perfect and pretending to be will lead to disappointment and resentment in the long run. Instead, accept your flaws and work to improve yourself.

Being true to yourself ultimately necessitates self-awareness, introspection, and courage. It entails acknowledging and accepting all aspects of yourself, including those that are difficult or uncomfortable to confront. The reward for living authentically is a greater sense of purpose, happiness, and fulfillment in life.

BEWARE OF MANIPULATIVE WOMEN: MYTHOMANIA & PSEUDOLOGIA FANTASTICA

Manipulative behavior can have a negative impact on mental health, both for the person exhibiting it and those who are subjected to it. Manipulation can take many forms, from subtle tactics to outright coercion, and it can occur in personal relationships, professional settings, and even in larger societal environments.

Some women who engage in manipulative behavior may be motivated by various factors, such as a desire for control, insecurity, fear, or a lack of empathy. These underlying issues can lead to multiple mental health issues, such as anxiety, depression, and personality disorders. Furthermore, manipulating others can often result in a cycle of guilt and shame, exacerbating mental health issues.

My wife and I were confronted with a shocking revelation last year that would forever alter our perception of a family member. It all started when we discovered that someone close to my wife was using her tragic childhood abuse, which she had confided in only a few people, as a story of their own. This family member had been using my wife's painful past to manipulate unsuspecting men as a way to form an emotional bond.

My wife had suffered tremendously as a child, she had been raped and beaten by both her uncle, and her mother's boyfriend. My wife endured unimaginable abuse that had left deep emotional scars. She gradually gained the courage to tell her story to those family members she trusted, seeking solace and support. It was a huge challenge for her to open up about her trauma, but it was also a necessary step toward healing.

This family member saw an opportunity to profit from my wife's vulnerability. Motivated by her own desire for validation and a twisted need for control, this person began spinning a web of lies, fabricating her own story of childhood abuse that closely mirrored my wife's. She began conversing with men, strategically inserting fragments of my wife's story as her own and capitalizing on the intense emotions it evoked. Over the years, she has put together a complex story to elicit sympathy and form an emotional bond with these unsuspecting men.

When my wife was made aware of this information, it devastated her. This not only stirred up feelings of anger and betrayal, but it triggered her symptoms of PTSD which resulted in a psychotic episode. In January of 2023, my wife had to be hospitalized for several days and heavily medicated once again.

The consequences of manipulative behavior can be damaging. Manipulation can erode trust, foster feelings of helplessness and confusion, and exacerbate anxiety, depression, and trauma. While most of us have occasionally engaged in being untruthful or telling a "little white lie" some women have used manipulation as a consistent and deliberate strategy to achieve their goals.

Some women can exert control over men through a variety of means, including:

❖ Emotional manipulation:

To gain control over a man, some women may use sympathy, guilt, fear, or other emotions. For example, she may use emotional blackmail to get what she wants.

❖ Gaslighting:

Gaslighting is a tactic in which a woman attempts to make a man question their reality or perception of events. Gaslighting is harmful because it can make you feel insane or paranoid.

❖ Passive Aggressive Behavior:

Some women may use indirect communication or subtle actions to get what they want through passive-aggressive behavior. For example, she may use sarcasm or backhanded compliments to make someone feel bad.

❖ Positive reinforcement:

To get what they want, some women may use praise, flattery, or other forms of positive reinforcement. While positive reinforcement can be a healthy motivator, manipulators may use it to instill a sense of obligation or debt.

❖ Blame Shifting:

Some women may attempt to shift blame for their actions onto others. For example, she may blame her bad behavior on the actions or circumstances of you or other people.

I want to emphasize that <u>I'm in no way, shape or form making a blanket statement about women.</u> But it is imperative that you understand there are some women who may use lies to form an emotional bond with you.

It's also critical to recognize the signs that your partner may be using false and or exaggerated accusations of abuse to exert control over you. These may include accusing you of abuse without evidence, being overly emotional or dramatic about minor incidents, and threatening you with false accusations to get what they want.

Constantly seeking attention or sympathy, changing their stories frequently, portraying themselves as victims, and making grandiose claims about their experiences or accomplishments could indicate that a woman is lying to create an emotional bond. They may also be overly charismatic and charming but have few close relationships or meaningful connections with others.

You must be cautious and considerate if you suspect someone is lying to form an emotional bond with you. Do not dismiss your intuition or gut feeling because it can be a valuable tool in detecting manipulative behavior. It's also critical to establish boundaries and communicate your concerns. Be clear about your expectations and standards, and resist being manipulated or controlled. Seek help from trusted friends, family members, or mental health professionals if necessary and remember; get to know someone and observe their actions and behaviors before becoming sexually or emotionally involved.

It's important to remember that not every woman who engages in manipulative behavior does so on purpose, and most men may be unaware that they are being manipulated. If you are in a relationship with someone and suspect manipulative behavior, setting boundaries and seeking help from a therapist or trusted friend is vital.

Next, I will discuss manipulative behavior through the lens of two mental health disorders: Mythomania and Pseudologia

Fantastica. Although these conditions can affect both men and women, I'll address them from my personal experience as a man for the purposes of this book.

MYTHOMANIA

Mythomania is a psychological disorder characterized by a strong desire to tell lies or makeup stories, even when there is no apparent reason to do so. People with this disorder frequently lie compulsively and may struggle to distinguish between truth and fiction. Pathological lying or pseudologia fantastica are other terms for mythomania. Mythomania is classified as an impulse control disorder because people with it may feel compelled to lie even when it is unnecessary.

Mythomania may have the following warning signs:

- ✓ Exaggeration of accomplishments or abilities on a regular basis.
- ✓ Telling grandiose or elaborate stories that appear unlikely.
- ✓ Maintaining consistency in stories or lies becomes difficult.

- ✓ Making up excuses or reasons for behavior or actions on a regular basis.
- ✓ Difficulty admitting and accepting responsibility for mistakes or failures.
- ✓ Lying even when it is not necessary or advantageous to do so.
- ✓ Displaying no remorse or guilt for deception or lying.
- ✓ When confronted with inconsistencies, becoming defensive or aggressive.

As you can see, this can be a complex condition to manage, with severe consequences for the person's relationships and overall well-being. Here are some ways you can assist someone who is suffering from mythomania:

- ❖ Educate yourself about mythomania:

Understanding the condition is the first step in helping someone who has it. Learn about the causes, symptoms, and treatment options to better assist them.

- ❖ Encourage honesty:

When you catch someone lying, it's tempting to call them out or express your frustration. However, this frequently worsens the situation. Instead, gently encourage honesty and create a safe environment for them to be honest.

❖ Don't enable their behavior:

While being supportive is important, it's also essential not to enable someone's mythomania. This includes not covering for them or making excuses for their actions.

❖ Provide emotional support:

People suffering from mythomania frequently experience feelings of inadequacy or low self-esteem. Provide emotional support and tell them you care about them despite their lies.

❖ Encourage professional help:

Mythomania can be a complex condition to overcome, and it frequently necessitates the assistance of a professional. Please encourage them to seek therapy or counseling and offer to assist them in locating a suitable professional.

❖ Be patient:

Overcoming mythomania is a process that requires patience. Change takes time, so offer your encouragement and support throughout the journey.

It is important to note that not everyone who tells a lie suffers from mythomania. Mythomania is a severe and chronic condition that can significantly impact a person's life and relationships. If you suspect that you or someone you know suffers from mythomania, you must seek professional help.

Mythomania is typically treated with psychotherapy and medication, such as antidepressants or anti-anxiety medications. The treatment goal is to assist individuals in managing their compulsive lying and developing healthier coping mechanisms for dealing with stress and anxiety.

PSEUDOLOGIA FANTASTICA

Pseudologia fantastica is a psychological term that describes a pattern of behavior in which an individual tells lies regularly, often to the point where they believe their lies. Pathological lying is another term for this type of behavior.

The term "Fantastica" refers to the elaborate and imaginative nature of lies told by people suffering from pseudologia fantastica. These lies may be said for various reasons, including gaining attention, improving their self-image or status, avoiding punishment or negative consequences, or simply for entertainment or pleasure.

People suffering from pseudologia fantastica may be skilled at deception and capable of maintaining their lies for extended periods. However, as time passes, their lies may become more elaborate and/or challenging to maintain, leading to feelings of guilt, shame, or anxiety.

It is critical to understand that pseudologia fantastica is a behavioral pattern, not a diagnosis or specific mental health condition. However, it is frequently associated with other mental health conditions, such as borderline or narcissistic personality disorder.

Here are some examples of pseudologia fantastica:

- ✓ A person claims to have a photographic memory, perfectly recalling every detail of their life.
- ✓ A person tells a story about surviving a dangerous situation, such as becoming lost in the wilderness or narrowly avoiding a car accident. However, further investigation reveals that their version of events is only partially accurate.
- ✓ A person asserts that they have a prestigious job or education, such as being a high-level executive at a major corporation or obtaining a degree from a prestigious university. However, their story unravels when questioned about their qualifications or employment history.
- ✓ A person fabricates personal or professional accomplishments, such as claiming to have won a major sporting event or receiving a prestigious award. However, there is no evidence to back up these assertions.

While pseudologia fantastica involves habitual lying, it is not the same as pathological lying, which is frequently associated with underlying psychological or neurological conditions.

Helping someone with these conditions can be difficult, but here are some techniques to help you navigate the situation:

❖ Avoid confrontation:

Confronting someone who suffers from mythomania or pseudologia fantastica can elicit defensive behavior and exacerbate the situation. Instead, approach the individual with empathy and understanding.

❖ Validate their emotions:

People suffering from mythomania or pseudologia fantastica may tell lies to cope with feelings of inadequacy, low self-esteem, or anxiety. Recognize their emotions and assist them in discovering healthier ways to deal with them.

❖ Concentrate on the present:

People suffering from these conditions may embellish or exaggerate their past experiences. Refocus the conversation on current events and situations.

❖ Be patient:

It takes time and effort to change compulsive lying behavior. To encourage positive change, be patient and consistent in your support.

❖ Encourage therapy:

Mythomania and pseudologia fantastica are both mental illnesses that can benefit from therapy. Encourage the individual to seek professional assistance and provide support throughout the process.

❖ Avoid enabling:

Do not draw attention to or reinforce the person's lies. Instead, please encourage them to tell the truth and reward them when they do.

To assist someone suffering from mythomania or pseudologia fantastica, patience, empathy, and a willingness to support them through professional therapy and healthier coping mechanisms are required. Patience, understanding, and a desire to offer emotional support are necessary. You can help them manage their condition and live a happier, healthier life by learning about it, encouraging honesty, and offering support.

Chapter 2
NAVIGATING MARRIED LIFE

HOME IS WHERE ~~THE HEART~~ YOUR WIFE IS

Have you ever heard someone say, home is where the heart is? Although it may sound like a common phrase, "home is where the heart is" carries a powerful message. This saying emphasizes that our sense of Home is determined not just by a physical place or building but by its associated individuals and emotions.

Allow me to provide you with a few examples that illustrate the meaning of the phrase:

❖ A Place of Love and Belonging:

Home is where we experience the warmth of love and a deep sense of belonging. It's the space where we can be our authentic selves, surrounded by loved ones who accept us for who we are. It's a place where we can express our emotions freely, find comfort, and build precious memories with those who matter most.

- ❖ Emotional Connection:

The phrase suggests that Home is not just a physical entity; it resides in our hearts. It symbolizes our emotional connection with our loved ones and the memories we create together. It's the laughter, the tears, and the shared experiences that make a place truly feel like Home.

- ❖ Safety and Security:

Home is a refuge from the world's chaos. It's a place where we feel safe, protected, and at ease. It's where we can let our guard down, unwind, and recharge our spirits. The comfort and security we find at Home allow us to face life's challenges with renewed strength.

- ❖ Familiarity and Roots:

Home gives us a sense of understanding and roots. It's where we often find our family traditions and cultural identity. It's a place that holds the echoes of our past, shaping our present and influencing our future. Home grounds us and reminds us of who we are and where we come from.

- ❖ Unconditional Love:

Above all, "home is where the heart is" embodies the power of love. It's a reminder that the love we share with our family, friends, and loved ones makes a place feel like Home. It's a love that is unwavering, unconditional, and capable of nurturing our souls.

So, you see, Home is a place where you feel safe, loved, and cherished. It's a haven where you can be authentic without fear or judgment. For me, that place isn't just a physical structure with walls and a roof; it's my beautiful wife's loving arms and warm smile.

My wife is the epitome of Home for me. From the moment we met, she captured my heart and transformed my world in the most profound way. Her unconditional love and unwavering support have given me a sense of security and contentment that I never thought possible.

Looking into her eyes, I see a reflection of our shared dreams, laughter, and endless adventures. Her love has become the foundation upon which I build my life, and her presence brings a comforting familiarity that can't be matched.

My wife is the heartbeat that resonates within me, a constant reminder that no matter where we are, I am home as long as I'm with her. Her love has built the four walls around us into a place of warmth, compassion, and unwavering affection.

I often thank my wife for being the foundation on which our love flourishes. With her, I feel safe to be vulnerable and to share my deepest fears and highest aspirations. She has created an environment where my heart can thrive and I am eternally grateful for that. As we journey through life together, I am filled with gratitude for the incredible woman she is. She has given me a home within her heart, and I promised to protect it with every ounce of my being.

So men, next time you encounter the phrase "home is where the heart is," remember that it's not just about bricks and mortar; it's about the emotional connection with your wife and her sense of belonging that transform a physical space into a cherished home. Embrace your wife wholeheartedly and create a home where your heart can thrive.

THE ART OF LOVE IN MARRIAGE

Marriage is a sacred bond that requires effort, commitment, and much love. We must remember that marriage is a two-way street and it's not just about us, it's about our wives too. It's essential to learn how to love your wife. And not just any love, but a selfless, patient, and understanding love.

I used to think that saying "I love you" was enough to express my feelings in the early stages of my relationship. However, I later realized that love is more than just words. Love is a verb and it necessitates actions that reflect the depth of those feelings.

My experiences have taught me that love isn't just about grand gestures; it also has the potential to be found in everyday events. It entails being there for one another through ups and downs, as well as being patient, forgiving, and selfless. This type of love in a marriage takes time, effort, and a willingness to grow together.

If you have had difficulty understanding the true nature of love in a marriage, here are some examples that may assist you.

❖ It strengthens your bond:

Building a solid and lasting foundation with your wife involves learning to love her. Love is the foundation of any successful marriage, and expressing love towards your wife strengthens your bond.

❖ It makes her feel valued:

It's essential for women to feel valued, appreciated, and loved. When you love your wife, she feels she holds an important place in your life. You must demonstrate that you care about her and that she is your top priority.

❖ It improves communication:

In any relationship, it is vital to prioritize communication. When you love your wife, you are more inclined to actively listen to her, comprehend her needs, and communicate effectively. This opens the door to better communication between the two of you.

❖ It sets a good example:

As a husband, setting a positive example for your children is crucial to demonstrating love and respect toward your spouse.

When children witness their parents exhibiting loving and respectful behavior towards one another, they are more likely to adopt similar behavior in their relationships with people.

❖ It leads to a happier marriage:

When you learn how to love your spouse, your marriage is happier. A joyful marriage is characterized by both partners feeling loved, valued, and respected. Therefore, it is essential to prioritize being a loving partner to your wife rather than just focusing on the concept of marriage itself.

Marriage is more than a legal agreement; it is a bond between two individuals who share love and respect for one another. As men, we must express our support and affection for our wives by backing up our words with our actions. Don't just tell her you love her; show her you love her.

Don't get bogged down by societal expectations, strive to be your best. You should aim to be the rock that your wife can always rely on, providing her with emotional support, love, and understanding. By being a stable foundation in her life, you can help her navigate whatever challenges come her way.

Don't allow the institution of marriage to define your role as a husband; instead, "become the institution" for your wife after marriage. Be there for her when she needs you, support her dreams and aspirations, and always treat her with love and respect. Be patient, kind, and understanding, even in adversity.

THE BLUEPRINT

It's important to remember that marriage is not solely about finding the perfect partner, it's also about striving to be the perfect partner yourself. So, try to be the kind of husband your significant other deserves, someone who truly loves and supports them through life's ups and downs.

ABANDON THE 50/50 MENTALITY

Marriage is a partnership built on mutual trust, respect, and commitment, and it requires both partners to contribute to the relationship to make it work. Splitting everything 50/50 may seem fair and logical, but a better approach exists. The key to a successful marriage is giving 100%, not just 50%.

It's easy to keep score in your marriage when approaching it with a 50/50 mindset. Both partners begin to calculate who has done what and who owes whom. This fosters a competitive environment, which can lead to resentment and frustration, and it fails to consider individual strengths and weaknesses, which can be unhealthy for any relationship.

There will be occasions when one partner must contribute more than the other. For example, if one partner deals with a difficult situation, such as an illness or job loss, the other may need to step up and take on additional responsibilities. This can lead to tension and resentment in a 50/50 marriage. It is critical to recognize that there will be times when one partner must give more and must be willing to do so without keeping a score.

This was the situation I found myself in when my wife was diagnosed with PTSD, Bipolar disorder, and major depressive disorder. She has been hospitalized frequently over the years and has been heavily medicated at times, preventing her from performing simple household tasks or working outside of the home.

If I had the 50/50 mentality, I would have added tension to an already difficult situation by harboring resentment for feeling obligated to pick up her slack. Instead, I had previously embraced the 100% mindset earlier in our marriage. With this mindset, I was able to properly love and care for my wife during her time of need, as well as manage our finances and run the household.

I understand it is not uncommon for one spouse to believe they contribute more than the other. In this case, it is critical to remember that even if your wife can only contribute 50%, giving 100% will benefit your marriage and this is why:

❖ It establishes the tone for your relationship:

By giving 100%, you set the tone for your relationship. It demonstrates your dedication to making the marriage work and your willingness to put forth the necessary effort. Your spouse will notice your commitment and be inspired to reciprocate.

❖ It strengthens your bond:

By giving 100%, you will strengthen your bond with your wife. She will feel more connected to you if you show her love and appreciation. This will assist you in overcoming any obstacles that may arise.

❖ It fosters a positive environment:

By giving 100%, you can foster a positive environment in your home. Your wife will feel loved, appreciated, and respected, leading to a happier and healthier environment for both of you.

❖ It results in a more satisfying marriage:

A successful marriage requires effort on the part of both partners. You are more likely to have a satisfying marriage if both of you put in 100% effort. You will feel more content if you try to keep your spouse happy.

As you can see, one of the best gifts you can give your wife is to love her completely, 100% of the time. It demonstrates to her that you're serious about your relationship and that you mean what you say. Not only will it help you build a stronger bond with her, but it will also lead to greater intimacy and understanding. This kind of selflessness is rare and beautiful, but it will enrich both of your lives.

I know firsthand how challenging it can be to love someone unconditionally. Disagreements and opposing viewpoints will arise, and you may face challenges that put your relationship to the test. However, if you remain committed to unconditionally loving your wife, you can overcome these challenges together and emerge even more robust.

So, start demonstrating to your wife how important she is in your life and commit to making her feel cherished and loved. Remember, when you unconditionally love your wife, you will eventually reap the benefits of a positive and satisfying relationship.

YOUR WIFE VS YOUR SPORTS

Like many men I know, sports are enjoyed and used to unwind and take a break from the daily routine. Whether you enjoy basketball, football, boxing, MMA, soccer, golf or hockey, sports can be an excellent outlet for relaxation. Moreover, participating in sports can be something that allows you to connect with others and build relationships with friends, family, and colleagues. Whether you attend games, or participate in fantasy leagues, you can develop a sense of camaraderie and companionship. However, it is essential to remember that spending too much time on sports-related activities can sometimes cause you to neglect your marital obligations.

Over the years, many young men have expressed their frustration to me explaining that their wives hate sports and give them a difficult time on gameday. They ask me if my wife allows me to watch football uninterrupted. My response is always yes, but they seem skeptical. So, I ask these young men, "have you thought about the possibility that your wife doesn't dislike sports, but might feel left out or overshadowed by the amount of attention and importance you give to them?"

Their silence is always golden, so I continue, "take a moment to put yourself in her shoes and think about how your actions and priorities might be making her feel. Ask yourself if you are unintentionally conveying that sports are more important to you than your commitment to her. By reflecting on these things, you can better understand and empathize with her point of view."

I explain to these young men that although I'm engrossed in a game, boxing match, or any other sport, my wife can request something, and I'll attend to her needs, no matter how big or small. However, I treat her with this level of respect daily, not only during game day. By demonstrating to my wife that she can approach me at any time without being a burden, she reciprocates by allowing me to watch the game in peace and often joins me.

It's amazing to see the expression on their faces when they finally realize how something so simple can be easily missed amidst the excitement of the football season. It's like a lightbulb goes off in their mind, and it's priceless.

Men, you can't let your excitement for the game allow you to forget to create an environment of trust and understanding with your wife, it's crucial to acknowledge and validate her feelings. Try to create a supportive environment by showing genuine interest in your wife's hobbies and activities. Encourage her interests with the same level of enthusiasm you have for the game, this will promote equality and understanding.

Also, gradually introduce your wife to the aspects of sports that you enjoy. Participate in sports-related activities together, like attending games or watching matches at home. By sharing your passion and experiences, you can deepen your connection and help her understand why sports are important to you.

Remember, for a fulfilling relationship, it is important to understand, compromise, and support each other. If you feel like sports may be taking priority over your wife, try to recognize and address those feelings. Open communication, empathy, and shared values can help ensure that your love for sports and your love for your wife can coexist harmoniously.

EMOTIONS ARE NOT ONLY FOR WOMEN

Do you ever feel like society expects you to express anger more than you express sadness or disappointment? Sometimes, it's difficult or uncomfortable for us to show emotions of sadness, so we end up being angry and aggressive. Unfortunately, this has become a pattern of how we've learned to express ourselves, and it's not healthy for ourselves or others. That's why it's important to learn how to manage our anger in a positive way.

Men, please understand that we have emotions also and one emotion that plagues us is anger. While it is essential to recognize that no man or woman experiences and processes emotional anger in the same way, some general differences are worth exploring.

How we communicate our feelings is one of the primary ways men and women process anger differently. Consider the last time your relationship went through a rough patch. If your woman was upset, she may have cried, yelled, or expressed herself in an emotional way. If you were angry, you might have withdrawn, gone silent, or, in some unfortunate cases, become violent and lashed out at someone or something.

Another distinction between us and women when it comes to emotional processing is how we deal with stress and difficult situations. We may be more likely to use avoidance as a coping mechanism, whereas our wives may seek social support and talk through their feelings with others.

For example, if a woman is stressed at home, she may be more likely to talk about her feelings with friends or family members, seek support from a therapist or counselor, or engage in self-care activities such as exercise, meditation, or yoga. On the other hand, if a man is stressed at home, he may cope by working longer hours, engage in hobbies or activities that distract him from the stress, or even abuse alcohol or other substances to numb the pain.

In my book, In Love with My 5 Wives, I discuss a time in my life when I didn't know how to deal with my anger or emotions in a healthy manner. I turned to hard liquor to numb my feelings because I was angry, stressed out, and going through a lot of emotional turmoil. When the alcohol was no longer enough to mask my pain, I attempted suicide by swallowing a handful of pills and drinking a bottle of vodka.

Men, please understand that anger is a natural emotion that can be challenging to deal with. Uncontrolled anger can harm your relationship leading to conflict, quarrels, and resentment, and it can also result in physical and emotional abuse, neither of which is acceptable.

Learning to manage your anger positively is critical to avoid these adverse outcomes. Here are some things that may help you:

❖ Determine your triggers:

List the situations, people, or events that make you angry. Understanding what makes you angry can help you develop coping strategies before your emotions spiral out of control.

❖ Take a step back:

If you notice yourself becoming angry, step back and calm down. This could include taking a few deep breaths, walking, or relaxing, reading or listening to music.

❖ Communicate openly:

If something bothers you, you must express your feelings calmly and respectfully. Avoid yelling or calling people names; focus on articulating your concerns and needs.

- ❖ Practice Empathy:

Try to see things through your partner's eyes. This can help you understand why they are acting how they are, allowing you to approach the situation with compassion and understanding.

- ❖ Psychological Therapy:

Consider consulting with a therapist if you're having trouble controlling your anger. A mental health professional can help you explore the root causes of your anger and develop coping strategies, and they can give you tools to help you deal with your emotions in a healthy way.

- ❖ Learn to communicate assertively:

Rather than destructively expressing your anger, learn to communicate your needs and feelings assertively.

- ❖ Seek help from loved ones:

Speak with friends and family members who can offer emotional support and encouragement.

- ❖ Join a support group:

Consider joining a group of men dealing with similar anger issues, as this can provide a sense of community and accountability.

- ❖ Practice forgiveness:

Let go of grudges and resentments that may fuel your anger, and practice forgiveness towards yourself and others.

❖ Set boundaries:

Recognize the situations and people that make you angry and set firm boundaries to protect your emotional well-being.

❖ Learn to manage your time effectively:

Feeling overwhelmed and stressed can trigger anger, so prioritize self-care and manage your time effectively.

❖ Create a self-care routine:

Schedule time for activities that bring you joy and help you relax, such as listening to music, going for a drive, or spending time with loved ones.

❖ Avoid substance abuse:

Drugs and alcohol can exacerbate anger, so avoid using them as a coping mechanism.

You can improve your marriage and overall quality of life by positively managing your anger. Remember that anger is a normal emotion; how you deal with it matters.

So, take the time to understand your triggers, practice self-control, communicate openly, and practice empathy, and if you are one of the men who has tried one or more of these techniques but still find it difficult to control your anger, take a deeper look into obtaining psychological therapy.

SOME PRACTICAL ADVICE FOR YOUR FUTURE TOGETHER LIFE INSURANCE + ESTATE PLANNING: A WILL AND TRUST FUND

LIFE INSURANCE

In my city, it's common to see people holding signs on street corners or outside of shopping malls, soliciting donations to cover the funeral costs of a loved one. It breaks my heart to see people in such a desperate situation. This was the situation I found myself in when I saw my wife holding a sign, desperately trying to raise funds for her sister's funeral arrangements.

The scene was heartbreaking. My usually composed and strong wife was visibly shaken and vulnerable. She had lost her sister, someone she loved and cherished; not only was she unable to properly grieve, but she was now overwhelmed with the burden of raising enough money to give her a proper burial. I felt utterly helpless, unable to alleviate her suffering or resolve the situation.

That's when I realized how important it is for men to step up and be there for their loved ones when they need us the most. It also served as a reminder of the financial difficulties that many families face when a husband or parent does not purchase life insurance.

As a husband, I'm sure you are deeply concerned about the well-being of your family. It is critical to ensure that your loved ones are cared for and secured both now and in the future. A way to ensure that security is to consider purchasing life insurance.

Life insurance is a financial safety net that can support your wife and children during your untimely death. Here are some of the reasons why every man should prioritize purchasing life insurance:

❖ It Will Protect Your Family's Finances:

If you passed away, your family would face financial consequences. Life insurance can provide a lump sum payment to your loved ones, which can be used to cover expenses such as funeral costs, outstanding debts, and ongoing living expenses.

❖ It Will Secure Your Children's Future:

If you have young children, life insurance can help secure their future. A life insurance policy payout can be used to cover the costs of education, childcare, and other expenses associated with raising children.

❖ It Gives You Peace of Mind:

Knowing that your family will be cared for in the event of your death will give you peace of mind. Life insurance can provide you with the security of knowing that your loved ones will be financially safe and capable of maintaining their standard of living.

❖ Concerns About Your Health:

Life insurance premiums rise with age, so purchasing it earlier can be advantageous if you are diagnosed with a medical condition.

❖ Flexibility:

Life insurance policies come in various forms, with varying levels of coverage, terms, and premium costs. You can tailor a policy to your specific needs and budget, ensuring you get the coverage you require at an affordable price.

In simple terms, purchasing life insurance is an essential step every man should take to ensure his family's financial security. It's never too early to start thinking about the future; life insurance can be valuable in achieving that goal. Don't put off protecting your loved ones until it's too late; so, take the first step today and purchase adequate life insurance.

ESTATE PLANNING: A WILL & TRUST

In addition to purchasing life insurance, it is critical to consider your future and what you wish to leave behind for your loved ones. Estate planning is one way to ensure that your wishes are carried out after your death. Estate planning entails devising a strategy for distributing your assets and having a Will and Trust is integral to that process.

A Will is crucial because it lets you specify how you want your assets distributed after passing away. Without a Will, your assets will be distributed under state law, which may not align with your wishes. For example, if you have children from a previous marriage and perish without a Will, your assets may go entirely to your current spouse, leaving your children with nothing.

This is where having a Will comes into play. A Will is a legal document that specifies how your assets will be distributed to your loved ones after you perish.

Here are a few advantages that come from having a Will:

❖ Control Over Your Assets:

One of the primary advantages of having a Will is that it allows you to direct how your assets are distributed. You can specify who will inherit your property, money, and other assets. Without a Will, your state's laws will dictate how your assets are distributed, which may not align with your wishes.

❖ Avoiding Family Disputes:

Having a Will in place may assist in avoiding family disputes. Without a Will, there may be clarity and disagreements about who should receive certain assets, adding stress and tension to an already stressful situation. A Will specifies how your assets should be distributed, reducing the likelihood of family conflict.

❖ Estate Taxes:

A Will can also assist in reducing estate taxes, which can significantly burden your heirs. You can reduce the taxes your estate will owe by specifying how your assets should be distributed.

❖ Peace of Mind

Finally, having a Will can give you and your loved one's peace of mind. You can ensure your wishes are fulfilled after your death by creating a plan for your assets. This can provide your family with comfort and security during a difficult time.

In addition to your Will, a Trust can offer additional advantages such as avoiding probate, lowering estate taxes, and ensuring privacy. Trusts can also provide for loved ones who cannot manage their finances, such as minor children or people with disabilities. As a husband, you must think about the future and take steps to protect your assets and loved ones.

These are the following examples of how a Trust can help in specific situations:

❖ Avoid Probate:

Probate is the legal process that distributes a person's estate after death. This can be a time-consuming and costly process that is often avoidable with a Trust. Assets in a Trust are not subject to probate, which can save your loved one's time, money, and stress.

❖ Protect Your Assets:

A Trust can help keep your assets safe from creditors, lawsuits, and other threats. You can protect your assets from these risks and ensure their preservation for your beneficiaries by transferring ownership of your assets to the Trust.

❖ Control Distribution:

When you use a Trust, you have more say over how your assets are distributed after you pass away. You can specify how and when your assets are distributed and appoint a Trustee to manage the Trust according to your wishes.

- ❖ Privacy:

A Trust is a private document, as opposed to a Will, which becomes a public record after your death. This means your personal affairs and assets can be kept confidential and out of the reach of prying eyes.

- ❖ Provide for Your Loved Ones:

A Trust can be a powerful tool for providing for your loved ones after you're gone. You can specify how much and when your beneficiaries receive distributions from the Trust. You can also create a plan to care for minor children or family members with special needs.

After establishing your Will and Trust documents, you must establish a Trust account with a bank. You can find information on how to do so by researching the steps online or by simply walking into a bank and speaking with a representative.

As you can see, estate planning ensures that your legacy and wishes are fulfilled after death. With a Will and Trust, you can ensure your assets are distributed according to your wishes and that your loved ones are provided for even when you are gone. So, make an estate plan reflecting your values and goals, and consult an experienced attorney who can guide you through the process.

Chapter 3
THE INFLUENCE OF ENVIRONMENT

THE WRONG ADVICE FROM THE "RIGHT MAN"

In my mid 20s, I was fortunate enough to land a promising career. It was a great position that offered endless possibilities for advancement. However, I gradually realized I was working alongside men with a pessimistic outlook on marriage.

These men, who were in their 40s and 50s, frequently discussed their dissatisfaction with marriage and expressed a desire to be single. They spoke negatively about their wives and often joked about "it's cheaper to keep her" referring to the idea that it is more financially beneficial to remain married rather than risk losing everything going through a divorce.

Initially, I considered it harmless teasing, I didn't know any better. After all, my biological father never played a role in my life, but I gradually began to understand how harmful their opinions were. Their pessimism started to affect my own life, and combined with my current struggles, it clouded my judgment regarding my relationship and dedication. I began to doubt the concept of marriage and whether it was worth the effort.

We must understand that taking advice from men who don't respect their wives can harm our relationship. When someone consistently surrounds themselves, listens to, or takes advice from people who lack respect for their partners, they may subconsciously adopt these attitudes and behaviors towards their significant other.

In addition, when men surround themselves with others who disrespect women, it can normalize this behavior and make it seem acceptable. This can create a toxic environment that perpetuates harmful attitudes and actions toward women.

Reflecting on the start of my career, I appreciate the valuable lessons I gained. I now understand the damaging effects of toxic perspectives and negative influences, which can get in the way of our ability to make sound judgments. It's crucial to seek positive results and guidance from men who prioritize their commitment to their spouse and marriage.

Surrounding yourself with men who have had successful marriages before you can be helpful. These men have likely faced similar situations to what you are currently experiencing or may face. By observing and learning from these types of men, you can acquire valuable knowledge on overcoming challenges and accomplishing your objectives more efficiently.

These men can also offer valuable guidance and support for your personal and professional growth. Additionally, they can inspire and motivate you by sharing their experiences of overcoming challenges and achieving success. Their example can help you stay focused on your own goals.

Of course, when choosing a mentor or role model don't take it lightly. Learn from someone who has achieved success and choose someone who can provide valuable insights, guidance, and inspiration to help you succeed in both personal and professional endeavors.

FROM MOMMA'S BOY TO HUSBAND PART 1

As a young boy, you were most likely referred to as a "momma's boy." You were probably close to your mother and relied on her for everything, and she was always there to offer advice, love, and support. As you age, you must accept that you must become more self-sufficient and take responsibility for yourself. It will not be easy, but it is necessary if you want to be a good husband and partner.

Not being a "momma's boy" does not imply turning your back on your mother. Having a healthy, supportive relationship with your mother is possible while developing your identity as a husband and making independent decisions.

If you are having trouble, here are some suggestions for striking a balance between independence and maintaining a close relationship with your mother:

❖ Communicate openly:

Discuss your goals, aspirations, and decisions with your mother. Be honest about your feelings and thoughts and listen to hers as well. Misunderstandings and conflicts can be avoided with effective communication.

❖ Set clear boundaries and stick to them:

It is critical to set clear boundaries and stick to them. Be respectful but firm in communicating what you are uncomfortable with.

❖ Accept responsibility:

Being self-sufficient entails accepting responsibility for your actions and decisions. Avoid blaming your mother for your problems and take responsibility for your choices.

❖ Show gratitude:

Remember to appreciate your mother for all the love and support she has given you. Expressing gratitude can strengthen your relationship and make her feel valued.

It may be difficult at first to break the patterns of your past and let go of your dependence on your mother. But as you get to know your wife better, you'll realize you can trust her just as much as you've grown to trust your mother. Remember, your wife is your partner, your equal, and someone you can rely on, and over time, you will learn to be there for her in ways you have never been for anyone else. You can support her through life's ups and downs, offer advice and guidance, and listen when she needs it most, just as your mother did for you.

FROM MOMMA'S BOY TO HUSBAND PT. 2

If your mother disapproves of your wife, you may feel trapped in a difficult situation. On the one hand, you want to keep a positive relationship with your mother, but you also want to stand up for your wife and maintain a healthy relationship with her.

It's critical to recognize that your mother may have reasons to dislike your wife. Maybe she thinks your wife isn't good enough for you, or perhaps she's just having trouble adjusting to the fact that you're starting a family of your own. Whatever the reason, it is critical to recognize and respect your mother's point of view.

While acknowledging your mother's feelings is essential, so is setting boundaries. Make it clear that you love and respect your wife and that negative comments or behavior toward her are unacceptable. When communicating these boundaries to your mother, be firm but respectful.

❖ Communicate openly and honestly:

Communication is essential in any relationship, but it is imperative when dealing with family dynamics. Please discuss with your mother why she dislikes your wife and try to understand her point of view. Simultaneously, be open with your mother about how her behavior affects you and your wife.

❖ If necessary, seek therapy:

If you find it challenging to handle this problem alone, you should seek outside assistance. This could take the form of a therapist or counselor who can assist you in processing your emotions and creating a plan of action to handle the circumstance.

Remember, your wife is your life partner, and you must prioritize your relationship with her. At the same time, even if your mother dislikes your wife, you can maintain a positive relationship with her. You can work through this challenging situation and find a solution that works for everyone involved if you communicate openly, honestly, and respectfully.

FROM MOMMA'S BOY TO HUSBAND PT. 3

If you discover your mother dislikes your wife, and now your mother is attempting to manipulate your father into siding with her, you have your work cut out for you! Battling your mother is difficult enough, but battling both parents? Damn!

Getting married is supposed to be an exciting and joyful experience. Do not let your parents deprive you of this opportunity. It will already be a difficult transition for you from being a son to being a husband. One of the most difficult challenges you may face is letting go of your parents or having your parents let go of you so that you can fully embrace your new wife.

According to the Bible, a man will leave his father and mother and be joined to his wife, and the two will become one flesh. This verse, found in Genesis 2:24, emphasizes the importance of leaving one's parents and starting a new family with one's wife.

While it is important to cherish and maintain relationships with your parents, your primary commitment must be honoring your wife. You should put your wife's needs ahead of your parents' and work hard to maintain a robust and healthy relationship with them. It will not be easy to let go of your parents, but it is necessary for the success of your marriage.

Here are some practical steps you can take to ease the transition:

❖ Set Boundaries:

Once again, you must establish clear expectations with your parents and set boundaries with them. Tell them that, while you love them, you are committed to building a solid marriage, which may necessitate prioritizing your spouse's needs over theirs. Setting boundaries is critical if your parents are excessively judgmental or intrusive. Tell them exactly what sort of behavior is acceptable and what is not. When communicating your limits, be firm but respectful.

❖ Communicate Openly:

When dealing with difficult parents, communication is essential. Being open and honest with them about your feelings, decisions, and plans is critical. Don't keep anything from them or avoid discussing important issues. Instead, be straightforward and specific about what you want and why you want it.

- ❖ Seek Wisdom:

Dealing with difficult parents can be stressful and overwhelming. As you navigate this transition, seek advice and guidance from trusted mentors or spiritual leaders, as they can provide helpful advice and support as you establish your new family unit.

When it's all said and done, you must remember, it is your life and your choice. While listening to and considering your parents' concerns is essential, you must do what is best for you. Don't let your parents make you feel guilty or pressure you into making disagreeable decisions. Maintain your position and be confident in your choices.

Interacting with difficult parents while getting married can be challenging, but you can successfully navigate this situation with the right attitude and strategies. Prioritizing your wife over your parents is a complex but necessary step in developing a healthy marriage. Remember that God is with you and will guide you every step of the way as you enter this new season of life.

IS RAP MUSIC INFLUENCING YOUR BEHAVIOR?

There is a widespread belief that rap music is the main influence on some young men's unfavorable attitudes and behaviors toward women. The truth is that a lack of positive male role models at home is probably a much more significant contributing factor.

A young man needs a positive male role model to develop positive attitudes and behaviors toward women. Such a role model can teach a young man how to respect women, treat them equally, and engage in healthy, constructive interactions. Lacking this guidance, young men may look to media—such as rap music—to learn how to treat women. Unfortunately, a large portion of the rap music that is currently popular frequently support sexist views and perpetuate negative stereotypes about women.

Many young men, like myself, are the products of dysfunctional homes with absent or uninvolved fathers, and it is important to realize that these young men are not the blame for this unfortunate reality. Young men might feel lost and unsure of how to interact with women if they do not have the guidance of a positive father figure and without this guidance, they may turn to the media, such as rap music, for guidance, even if that guidance is misguided.

Furthermore, the negative attitudes towards women often exhibited by young men who lack positive male role models can have significant consequences. Women may be treated poorly, subjected to harassment or abuse, and not given the respect they deserve, and this can have long-lasting effects on their self-esteem, mental health, and overall well-being.

Rap music, at times, has been singled out as a factor as to why some young men are disrespectful to women, but this is an oversimplified and unfair accusation. It's important to realize that while some rap music does contain misogynistic lyrics, these lyrics frequently reflect the realities of life in underprivileged, inner-city communities. Rap music can be viewed as a form of artistic expression that reflects the struggles and experiences of those who live in these communities rather than as something that incites disrespect.

I was a massive fan of rap music when I was a kid. The rhythms, rhymes, and storytelling all struck a deep chord with me. It was all I listened to, from early pioneers like Roxanne Shante, LL Cool J, The Beastie Boys, and Run DMC to later artists ranging from Kid "n Play, X Clan, and Public Enemy, all the way to artists like Too Short, E40, Mac Dre, and N.W.A. However, contrary to popular belief, rap music did not make me violent. It was the exact opposite; it assisted me in overcoming the trauma I had endured as a child.

I had a difficult time growing up. My mother and stepfather abused me physically, psychologically, and emotionally. I constantly lived in fear because I didn't know when the next attack would occur. I had no one to turn to for support because my biological father was absent.

Rap music evolved into my source of comfort during these difficult times. Nothing else could have communicated with me the way the lyrics did. They were unfiltered, sincere, and unrepentant. They did not sugarcoat life's realities; instead, they met them head-on. They discussed the difficulties of growing up in poverty, enduring racism, and losing loved ones. Understanding that I wasn't the only one going through such events comforted me.

So, no, rap music did not turn me into a violent person, nor did it alter my perception of how to treat women. Childhood abuse from my mother and stepfather and the absence of my biological father had the greatest impact on my life. We can help reduce the negative attitudes and behaviors toward women that are so prevalent today by providing young men with positive male role models who promote respect for women and healthy relationships.

BEING "WHIPPED" VS HONORING YOUR WIFE

Why does it seem like in our black and brown culture, especially with some the younger generation, when a man shows respect for his wife, he is considered to be whipped? If a man opens the car door for his wife, he is whipped. If a man contributes to household chores such as vacuuming the floors, washing dishes or doing laundry, he is whipped. Or if he simply pulls out a chair for his wife in a restaurant before he sits down, he is whipped.

I think we need to understand the phrase "whipped" which often refers to a man who does too much for and is too dominated by his wife. He may be perceived as weak or submissive, constantly doing what she says and failing to advocate for himself. It might be difficult for this man to achieve a balance between feeling "whipped" and honoring his wife. On the one hand, he wants to demonstrate his love and respect for his spouse by honoring her but doesn't want to feel dominated or controlled. So, how can he negotiate this tricky terrain?

Are you aware of how to distinguish between the two situations? If you struggle with finding balance and want to avoid feeling overly submissive, here are some things to keep in mind:

❖ Communication:

Communication is critical in any relationship, but it's imperative when it comes to striking a balance between being "whipped" and valuing your wife. If you believe your wife has too much power over you, you must voice your feelings politely. Engage in an open and honest discussion about your concerns and work together to find a solution that works for both of you.

❖ Respect:

It would help if you respected your wife in all aspects of your relationship to honor her. This entails carefully listening to her ideas, acknowledging her efforts, and respecting her as an equal partner. Being "whipped" on the other hand, involves giving up your goals and requirements to satisfy your wife's wishes.

- ❖ Compromise:

A healthy relationship requires both partners to compromise. If you're continuously caving into your wife's requests, it could be an indication that you're "whipped." However, if you and your wife are willing to compromise and find common ground, that signifies a mutually respectful relationship.

Some of you guys reading this book may argue and say, "according to the bible, a wife is expected to submit and obey her husband." While this is what the scripture states, it's remarkable how most of us focus solely on that aspect.

It's also crucial to remember that the Bible says, "husbands should love their wives like Christ loved the church and sacrificed himself for her."

Throughout history, there has been an ongoing theme of men honoring their wives at all costs, which was especially highlighted in the early twentieth century. During this time, men were expected to serve as protectors and providers for their families, and defending their wives was considered an honorable and essential aspect of fulfilling this role.

Due to this strong belief, men went to great lengths to honor their wives. Men were expected to defend their families' reputations, and any perceived threat to their wives' safety or reputation was viewed as a direct insult to their honor. This belief was deeply embedded in many cultures and was frequently accompanied by a sense of duty and chivalry toward one's wife. As husbands, we must prioritize honoring our wives. Honoring them entails treating them with dignity, listening to their concerns, and recognizing their contributions to our families and lives.

Regularly expressing gratitude, appreciation, and affection toward our wives is part of honoring them. This includes encouraging and assisting them in achieving their goals and dreams. We must demonstrate our love and devotion meaningfully while remaining faithful and committed to our relationship.

Unfortunately, our culture frequently portrays marriage and relationships negatively, implying that it is acceptable to mistreat or take our partners for granted. As men, we must reject this narrative and strive to have healthy and happy relationships with our wives.

So, let's put forth the effort and cultivate a culture of appreciation for our wives. They are our partners, companions, and allies and deserve to be treated with love, respect, and kindness. Honoring them lays a solid foundation for a satisfying and long-lasting relationship.

DON'T BE A HYPOCRIT

Let's talk about a critical issue in our culture that needs addressing, the hypocrisy of disrespecting women while demanding respect from the woman in your own life. It's time to reflect on our actions and consider how we treat others, particularly women. We need to recognize the glaring contradiction in our behavior and consciously try to change it.

Imagine this: You have a sister or a mother—a woman you love and deeply care about. You want the best for them and expect them to be treated with kindness, respect, and dignity. Now ask yourself, would you be comfortable with another man mistreating them? Would you stand idly by if they were subjected to disrespect, harassment, physical, mental or emotional abuse?

Chances are, your answer is a resounding "Hell No!" You would do anything to protect and defend them, ensuring they are treated with the utmost respect, not just because of who they may be related to, but because they are human beings and that's precisely how it should be.

If you read my first book, In Love with My 5 Wives, then you know I once suffered this problematic mindset. I mistreated my wife for years, yet I demanded her respect. However, in the chapter titled "My Epiphany," I took a hard look at myself and realized the root cause of my behavior. I had to retrain my thinking to understand that true respect is a steadfast principle and not just a convenient show.

So, let's dive in and explore why this is important:

❖ Respect for all women:

As men, it's essential to treat every woman with the respect and dignity they deserve. Whether it's our partners, family members, friends, colleagues, or strangers, we mustn't differentiate based on arbitrary factors like appearance, age, or social status. Genuine respect transcends these superficial boundaries and acknowledges the inherent worth of every individual.

❖ Equal opportunities:

We live in a society where women face challenges and inequalities. By being consistent in our respect, we actively support gender equality. It means promoting equal opportunities for women in every aspect of life—education, careers, leadership roles, and decision-making. Our actions should reflect the belief that women deserve the same chances to succeed and thrive.

❖ Active listening:

Consistency in respect means lending a listening ear to the voices of women. Their experiences, perspectives, and opinions are just as valid as ours. By actively listening and empathizing, we can better understand their challenges, contribute to meaningful conversations, and work together to create a more inclusive and fair society.

❖ Challenging harmful behavior:

Consistency also means speaking up against sexism, misogyny, and disrespectful behavior towards women. We shouldn't turn a blind eye, remain silent or be quick to pull out our cell phones, hit record, and watch unfair treatment or degrading attitudes. By actively challenging such behavior, we contribute to a safer and more supportive environment for everyone.

❖ Personal growth:

Consistently respecting women fosters personal growth and self-awareness. It requires introspection, understanding our biases, and unlearning harmful stereotypes. By continuously educating ourselves, we can identify and address our unconscious biases. Remember, growth is an ongoing process; we all have room to improve.

Respecting women starts with us; we need to check ourselves and hold each other accountable. Let's be conscious of our behavior and actions, ensuring they reflect our values. Let's strive to be men who champion and uplift women, and set an example for future generations.

Remember, how we treat our wives says much about who we are as men. Let's strive to be the man who empowers and respects the woman in our life and the women around us. Let's break the cycle of hypocrisy and create a world where women feel safe, valued, cherished and loved.

Chapter 4
HOW TO BE A SUPPORTIVE HUSBAND IN TOUGH TIMES

HOW TO SUPPORT YOUR WIFE THROUGH MENOPAUSE

Menopause is a natural biological process that typically occurs in a woman's late 40s or early 50s, marking the end of her reproductive years. Although menopause is a natural part of a woman's life, it can be difficult for her. Unfortunately, most of us men do not fully comprehend what our wives are experiencing during menopause, which can result in misunderstandings, frustration, and sometimes divorce.

My wife is 10 years older than I am, so when I was in my early 40s, she was in her early 50s, and that is when she began to struggle with Menopause. It began to cause a variety of physical and emotional changes in my wife that I did not understand. Hot flashes, night sweats, mood swings, anxiety, depression, and a decreased sex drive were among the symptoms that she was struggling with. These changes were physically and emotionally taxing on her, as well as myself, and it left us feeling isolated from one another and unsupported.

Unfortunately, at first, I became irritated by my wife's mood swings and I felt rejected by her diminished sex drive. I was simply unaware that my wife's body was undergoing significant changes that were beyond her control.

As you can see, this type of misunderstanding can cause tension and conflict in a marriage and unfortunately, in some cases, can lead to divorce. Many men may believe that their wife is no longer the person they married, and they may struggle to adjust to the changes brought on by menopause. However, we must understand that menopause is a natural part of life and that our wives need our love and support now more than ever.

As a husband, you can play a significant part in supporting your wife through menopause. Here are some of the things I did that can help you get started:

❖ Learn about menopause:

Menopause is a complex and commonly misunderstood stage of life. Take the time to educate yourself on the physical, emotional, and psychological changes that your wife may go through during this time. This knowledge will help you understand what she is going through and provide the appropriate level of support.

❖ Be patient:

Menopause can be a difficult time for women, causing them to become irritable, moody, and forgetful. Try to be patient and understanding when your wife is going through this difficult phase.

❖ Listen to her:

Listening to your wife is one of the most important things you can do for her during menopause. Encourage her to express her emotions, thoughts, and concerns, and tell her you support her.

❖ Help with housework:

Menopause can cause fatigue, making it challenging to keep up with daily household chores. Take on some of the tasks around the house, such as cooking, cleaning, or grocery shopping, to assist your wife.

❖ Support her self-care routine:

Menopause can be a time when women prioritize self-care. Allow your wife to take care of herself by encouraging her to engage in healthy habits like exercise, healthy eating, and meditation.

❖ Maintain a positive attitude:

Menopause can be an unpleasant experience but try to maintain a positive attitude. Concentrate on the positive change's menopause can bring, such as the end of menstrual cycles or the beginning of a new chapter in your life.

❖ Assist her in getting enough sleep:

Sleeping can be difficult during menopause due to hot flashes and night sweats. Assist your wife by keeping the bedroom cool, quiet, and comfortable. Consider purchasing high-quality mattresses, pillows, and bedding.

❖ Be patient when it comes to intimacy:

Menopause can affect a woman's libido, making sex uncomfortable or painful. Be patient and thoughtful of your wife's desires and requirements.

❖ Support her with medical care:

Menopause may lead to physical health issues that require medical attention. Accompany your wife to doctor's appointments and assist her in managing any medications she may be taking.

❖ Keep Communication Open:

Maintain open lines of communication with your wife. Encourage her to express her needs and concerns and guarantee that you support her through this trying period in her life.

It is critical to seek resources and support if your wife is going through menopause. Consult with your doctor or a menopause specialist. There are also numerous online resources, such as forums and blogs, where women can connect and share their experiences.

Finally, menopause can be a difficult time for you and your wife. While it may be tempting to give up on the relationship as things get complicated, you must remember that your wife needs your love and support now more than ever. With patience, understanding, and empathy, you can navigate this difficult time together and emerge stronger on the other side.

HOW TO SUPPORT YOUR WIFE THROUGH DEPRESSION

Depression is a complex mental health condition with numerous manifestations. While many people associate depression with feelings of sadness or hopelessness, it can also cause people to become irritable or angry. Depression and anger issues are frequently linked, and women who suffer from depression are likely to develop anger issues.

Depression can cause anger issues through a process known as emotional dysregulation. Women suffering from depression may become overwhelmed by negative emotions such as sadness, anxiety, or hopelessness. These intense feelings can be challenging to manage, and some women may become irritable or lash out in response.

Furthermore, depression can make women feel frustrated or powerless in their situation, and they may feel powerless over their lives, leading to rage or resentment toward themselves or others. For example, if your wife is suffering from depression and she cannot work due to her condition, she may become angry at you, her employer, or her coworkers for not understanding her difficulties.

Another way depression can lead to anger issues is through a process known as rumination. If your wife is depressed, she may become focused on negative thoughts or events from her past. This rumination can cause her to feel trapped in a negative thought cycle, leading to feelings of rage or frustration.

Depression can strike anyone, regardless of gender. However, there are some distinct ways depression can manifest in women.

For starters, women are more likely to suffer from depression due to hormonal changes during menstruation, pregnancy, childbirth, and menopause. Hormonal changes can impact mood and energy levels, and women may experience various symptoms, including sadness, irritability, and a lack of interest in daily activities.

Second, women frequently juggle responsibilities such as work, family, and housework, which can result in chronic stress and burnout. Chronic stress has been linked to the development of depression.

Third, women are more likely than men to obsess over negative thoughts and feelings, which can exacerbate depression symptoms. Women may also feel guilty or ashamed about their depression, which may keep them from seeking treatment.

We must recognize that depression is an illness, not a sign of weakness. If you notice a woman in your life exhibiting symptoms of depression, be supportive and encourage her to seek professional help. Depression treatment may consist of therapy, medication, or a combination of the two and can be very effective in managing symptoms and improving the overall quality of life.

If you're concerned about your wife's mental well-being and suspect that she might be going through depression, the following warning signs may be useful to you. However, it's important to remember that only a medical professional or specialist can accurately diagnose whether it's depression or another health condition.

- ☹ She's unusually quiet or remote
- ☹ She appears to be more easily annoyed or frustrated than usual
- ☹ She is easily distracted and disorganized
- ☹ She's not taking good care of her personal hygiene
- ☹ She's not as affectionate as she usually is

- ☹ She is not participating in activities she enjoys
- ☹ She's a little more emotional than usual
- ☹ She's not getting enough sleep
- ☹ She's not as motivated as she usually is
- ☹ She's not as sure as she used to be
- ☹ She is uninterested in resolving disagreements
- ☹ She is not looking for help from others
- ☹ She's not as outgoing
- ☹ She's not as grateful
- ☹ She's not as forgiving

You may also want to consider whether there have been any significant life changes or stressors. Significant life events, such as the death of a loved one, a job change, or a move, can frequently precipitate depression. Depression can make people more sensitive to criticism or adverse events, so keep an eye out for signs that she is taking things personally.

- ☹ Consider whether she is coping with substances:

People who are depressed may turn to drugs or alcohol to cope, so keep track of whether she is drinking more or using drugs. For instance, she could be drinking alone or more frequently than usual.

☹ Keep an eye out for suicidal thoughts or behaviors:

Because depression increases the risk of suicide, note if she expresses suicidal or self-harming thoughts. For example, she may feel hopeless or that life is not worth living.

☹ Consider whether she has a family history of depression:

Depression can run in families, so see if she has a history of depression.

This is not a complete list, but as you can see, there are many warning signs that your wife may be suffering in silence from depression. Encourage your wife to seek professional assistance from a licensed psychologist who can assist her in managing her symptoms and developing a treatment plan. Therapy, medication, or other interventions to help her cope with her depression may be included.

It is critical to remember that recovery from depression is a process, and your wife's feelings may improve gradually. Being patient, supportive and showering her with extra love as she goes through this difficult time is essential. Encourage her to put herself first and remind her that she is not alone.

HOW TO SUPPORT YOUR WIFE THROUGH PAST CHILD ABUSE TRAUMA

Knowing how to support your wife who has been a victim of child abuse can be challenging. It is critical to recognize that the consequences of child abuse can be long-lasting and complex, and that each survivor's journey is unique.

My wife is a survivor of atrocious and despicable child abuse. As I shared with you earlier, my wife was repeatedly molested, raped and beaten by one of her uncles and her mother's boyfriend and these facts were not revealed to me until 28 years into our relationship. My wife had been suffering in silence since childhood due to shame and embarrassment, and to put things into perspective, my wife was born in 1964, and the peak of her suffering did not occur until she was "triggered" in 2018 while attending college.

Supporting my wife through the deep wounds and trauma caused by her past child abuse was difficult, but seeing her strength and resilience has only strengthened my resolve to be there for her. Here's how I handled this delicate and difficult situation.

First and foremost, I made a strong effort to create a non-judgmental environment where my wife could share her experiences. I learned how to listen intently without interrupting or interjecting my thoughts. It was critical that she felt heard, validated, and understood.

I also learned about the effects of child abuse trauma, potential triggers, and the healing process. By learning more, I could empathize with my wife's emotions and reactions and provide her with appropriate support. I gently encouraged my wife to seek professional therapy. I found her a psychologist (Dr. Marchita Masters) to help my wife manage her feelings and navigate her trauma, and I accompanied her during every session, offering my support and reassurance.

Healing takes time and patience, and I realized my love and support were essential. I've learned to be understanding of my wife's progress, setbacks, and emotional swings. I've also tried to put myself in her shoes, reminding myself that her healing process is unique and necessitates empathy. I recognized the significance of providing my wife with consistent reassurance and validation. I reminded her that her past does not define her value or the love and support she deserves. I constantly affirmed her strength and admired her bravery in confronting her trauma.

It has also been critical for me to respect my wife's boundaries. I've learned to recognize when she needs space or time alone and I respected her need for privacy as she heals. Healing from trauma is a gradual process, and I've acknowledged and celebrated every small victory, fostering a sense of hope and resilience by recognizing and celebrating my wife's progress.

Above all, assisting my wife through her past child abuse trauma has necessitated unconditional love, patience, and dedication to her well-being. I remind myself that while I can't fix everything, I can be a rock of support, an advocate for her healing, and a loving presence by her side. We face these challenges together, celebrating the victories as we build a future filled with love, understanding, and growth.

HOW TO SUPPRT YOUR WIFE THROUGH PAST RELATIONSHIP ABUSE

I want to address a topic that holds great importance in any relationship: loving your wife through her past relationship hurts and or abuses. Relationships are complex, and our wives may carry emotional trauma from their past experiences. Questioning your role in fixing a problem you didn't cause is natural. However, it's essential to understand that supporting your wife is not about taking responsibility for the past but being her rock in the present.

First and foremost, it's crucial to acknowledge that you can't change the past. You didn't cause the hardship your wife experienced, and you cannot undo the pain inflicted upon her. Accepting this fact is not a sign of weakness but a recognition of reality. Feeling overwhelmed, confused, or unsure about your role in supporting her is okay.

When your wife shares her past relationship pain, lend her your ears without judgment or defensiveness. Create a space where she feels comfortable sharing her thoughts and emotions. Remember, she isn't blaming you for her past; she's seeking solace and understanding. Simply being present and listening attentively can make a world of difference.

When my wife was hospitalized in January and February of 2020, I listened without judgment as she shared her past abuses. I allowed her to express herself, validated her feelings and experiences, and let her know that her pain matters. I provided a safe and non-judgmental environment where she felt heard and understood.

I realized the wounds from my wife's past relationships, including our abusive past, required professional guidance. I encouraged my wife to seek therapy and counseling and I volunteered to participate with her if she felt it would benefit her healing process. She decided to give therapy a try and I actively participated in every therapy session, and when my verbal participation was not required, I actively listened.

During this time, I had to remember to take care of myself as well. Supporting my wife through her past relationship hurts was emotionally taxing at times. I engaged in self-care activities that recharged me and found support from my trusted psychologist when needed. Patience is critical and healing is not simple. Remember, setbacks are part of the journey.

Rebuilding trust is crucial, even if you were, or were not the one who broke it. Your unwavering support is paramount during this time. Assure your wife that she can rely on you for comfort, love, and understanding. Offer a shoulder to lean on, a hand to hold, and a heart that listens without reservation. Remind her that you are her partner, committed to standing by her side through thick and thin. Be consistent, reliable, and transparent in your actions. Trust is earned gradually; your steadfastness will help her heal and believe in love again.

HOW TO SUPPORT YOUR WIFE THROUGH PTSD

Post-Traumatic Stress Disorder (PTSD) is a mental health condition that can develop after experiencing or witnessing a traumatic event. Because of increased attention and concern for the mental health of Vietnam War veterans, post-traumatic stress disorder (PTSD) was initially thought to only affect combat veterans when it was first formally recognized as a diagnosis in the Diagnostic and Statistical Manual of Mental Disorders (DSM) in 1980. The disorder was initially given several names such as, "Shell Shock, Battle Fatigue and post-Vietnam syndrome" and was considered unique to combat veterans.

However, as research and clinical experience with PTSD grew, it became clear that anyone who had experienced or witnessed a traumatic event could be affected. Sexual or physical assault, natural disasters, car accidents, terrorist attacks, and other life-threatening situations are examples of traumatic events that can lead to PTSD.

Furthermore, PTSD can develop because of chronic stress or repeated trauma exposure, such as long-term domestic abuse. As a result, the diagnosis of PTSD is now accepted for anyone who has been exposed to a traumatic event or situation, regardless of whether they served in the military or not.

People with PTSD may experience a range of symptoms, including:

- Intrusive thoughts or memories of the traumatic event that they cannot control, including nightmares or flashbacks of the traumatic event that can be frightening and intense.
- Avoidance behaviors, such as avoiding people, places, or things that remind them of the traumatic event.
- Hyperarousal, or being constantly on edge; irritability; being easily startled; or having difficulty sleeping
- Negative thoughts or feelings, such as feeling guilty or ashamed, having a negative outlook on life, or losing interest in previously enjoyed activities.

It is critical to recognize that PTSD is a real and frequently debilitating condition that can affect anyone, regardless of age, gender, or background. While managing PTSD symptoms can be complex, many effective treatments, such as therapy and medication, are available.

As a husband, you must recognize that your wife's PTSD is not something she can "get over" or "move on" from. Instead, loved ones must be patient, understanding, and supportive to help them cope with their symptoms and work toward recovery. Encouraging them to seek professional help, if necessary, as well as being available to listen and provide emotional support, can go a long way toward assisting them in managing their condition and leading a fulfilling life.

Chapter 5
When to Seek Help

THE BENEFITS OF PSYCHOLOGICAL THERAPY

Most of us men are often reluctant to seek therapy for various reasons. Men are expected to be strong, independent, and stoic, which can create a stigma around seeking help for mental health issues.

However, from personal experience, I can tell you that therapy is essential for maintaining good mental health and well-being. Therapy has allowed me to discuss my problems and receive support and guidance from a trained professional. As I sit here today, I continue to see my psychologist once or twice a week, as I have done since late 2019. However, despite its numerous benefits, therapy has been stigmatized, particularly in our Black and Brown communities.

Many of our people regard mental health issues as a sign of weakness, and seeking professional help is often frowned upon. The stigma associated with mental health and therapy is deeply embedded in our culture and can be traced to several factors, including historical trauma, systemic racism, and cultural norms.

Slavery, colonization, and racism have all caused significant trauma to Black and Brown people throughout history. These traumas have resulted in a culture of resilience and self-sufficiency, where seeking assistance from outside sources is frequently regarded as a sign of weakness. Furthermore, our people have been subjected to discrimination and mistreatment within the healthcare system, leading to a lack of trust in mental health professionals.

Also, with most men in our communities, mental health issues are often viewed as a personal failing rather than a medical condition, and seeking help is sometimes considered a lack of faith in God. Furthermore, many of our people are often told to "suck it up" which can make it difficult for them to express their emotions or seek help when needed.

This stigma can have serious ramifications. It can deter people from seeking help, leading to untreated mental health issues, substance abuse, and even suicide. It can also perpetuate the trauma cycle and obstruct healing and growth.

Recognizing and addressing the stigma associated with therapy in our communities is critical. This can be accomplished through education, encouraging people to seek help when in need, and creating safe spaces where people can talk about their mental health and receive support without fear of judgment.

Fear of being judged or misunderstood by a therapist may contribute to men's reluctance to seek therapy. Men may be concerned that a therapist will not understand their feelings or will judge them for their actions or thoughts.

It's important to remember that seeking therapy is not a sign of weakness or failure and can benefit anyone suffering from mental health issues. Therapy can offer a safe and non-judgmental environment to explore and work through personal issues, improve communication skills, and develop coping strategies.

Now, let's talk about the advantages of psychological therapy and give some examples of how therapy can help you overcome common mental health issues.

❖ Stress and anxiety management:

Learning coping strategies to manage stress and anxiety is one of the most significant advantages of therapy. We are frequently exposed to high-pressure situations at work and in our personal lives, leading to chronic stress and anxiety. We can learn effective stress and anxiety management techniques in treatment, such as deep breathing exercises, mindfulness practices, and cognitive-behavioral techniques.

- ❖ Resolving Relationship Problems:

Relationship problems can be a significant source of stress and anxiety. Therapy can help us work through issues such as difficulty communicating with a partner, resolving conflicts, or ending a relationship. Therapy can help us improve our communication skills, set healthy boundaries, and work through the emotions associated with a breakup.

- ❖ Managing Depression:

Depression is a common mental health issue that affects men, but many men are ashamed or embarrassed to seek help. Therapy can provide a safe and non-judgmental environment to express feelings of sadness, hopelessness, and worthlessness. In treatment, men can learn coping strategies, such as cognitive-behavioral techniques, to help them manage their depression symptoms.

- ❖ Overcoming Trauma:

Many of us have experienced trauma, whether as a child or in the military. Trauma can have severe consequences for one's mental health, causing symptoms such as anxiety, depression, and post-traumatic stress disorder (PTSD). Therapy can assist men in dealing with trauma by providing a safe environment to process emotions and develop coping strategies to manage symptoms.

❖ Increasing Self-Esteem:

Men can benefit from therapy as well by increasing their self-esteem. Low self-esteem can lead to negative self-talk, self-doubt, and insecurity. Through treatment, men can learn to challenge negative beliefs and develop more positive self-talk. Therapy can also assist men in recognizing their own strengths and creating a more positive self-image.

Marriage won't always feel like a beautiful bond between two people; it can sometimes be challenging. When you marry, you agree to support your partner in sickness and health. Mental health is just as important as physical health, and you must understand the value of entering a marriage mentally prepared.

Anyone, regardless of gender, can suffer from mental health issues. Conversely, women are more likely than men to suffer from mental health disorders such as depression and anxiety. Women frequently suffer in silence, making it difficult for their partners to understand what they're going through. This is where mental toughness comes in. When you enter a marriage mentally prepared, you can better handle the ups and downs that will inevitably occur.

When you are mentally strong, you become more aware of your mental state, which will allow you to detect when something is wrong with your wife. If your wife has a mental illness, you must recognize the symptoms quickly to provide support.

It is also important to note that mental illness is not easily treatable and takes time, patience, comprehension and compassion. When you enter a marriage mentally prepared, you can better provide the support and care your wife requires. You can provide her with comfort and stability, making all the difference in her recovery.

So become mentally strong. It will help you maintain a healthy relationship as well as support your wife. It is critical to be able to communicate effectively as well as manage your own emotions. When mentally strong, you can handle conflicts more effectively and find solutions that work for both of you.

CONCLUSIONS

MEN, LEARN HOW TO SAY I LOVE YOU

The notion that men don't have to say "I love you" is a social construct perpetuated by gender roles and societal expectations. On the other hand, expressing love and affection is not a gendered behavior, and everyone should feel free to express their feelings in an authentic and meaningful way.

There is no inherent reason why men should not verbally express their love, and it is critical to dispel preconceptions, and I encourage you to verbalize your emotions openly and honestly. Love is a human emotion that should be freely celebrated and expressed without restrictions or expectations.

Growing up without my biological father was difficult, mainly because he was not around to express or verbalize his love and affection for me. For many years, I have given advice and counsel to many men, particularly young men, and I have often been told that hearing the words "I love you" from their father would have been a powerful and affirming experience and the absence of those words left a lasting impression.

Growing up without emotional validation can leave an empty space in your heart, but it's important to remember that love can take many forms. Just because your father was unable to express his love verbally is not an indication that he did not love you in his own unique way.

Perhaps he demonstrated his love by working hard to provide for the family or being there for you in times of need. It's critical to recognize these gestures and acknowledge the love shown to you, even if it hasn't been expressed in the way you had hoped.

It's never too late to start showing love and affection to others, including your family. You can make a better future for yourself and your loved ones by breaking the cycle of emotional detachment. I want you to know that saying "I love you" to your friends and family is acceptable. It is okay to hug your friends and express your support for them; it is okay to cry and express your emotions.

I understand how difficult it can be to break free from the norms and expectations that have been imposed on us, but we must. We create deeper connections and stronger relationships by expressing our love and emotions to one another.

So, my brothers, let me say it: I LOVE YOU. Let us support and uplift one another as we break free from the limitations imposed on us by society and previous broken generations.

PRAYER

Whatever religion you follow, whatever denomination you belong to, whatever divine being you believe in... pray.

Prayer is a practice that can be found in a wide range of religious and spiritual traditions. It entails communicating with or thinking about a higher power or deity, expressing gratitude, asking for guidance, and seeking assistance or support. Some studies have found that prayer can improve mental health by reducing symptoms of depression and anxiety and increasing overall well-being. It may also have physical health benefits, such as lowering blood pressure and reducing stress. It is critical to note that prayer should not be viewed as a replacement for medical or psychological treatment. However, it can be a complementary practice that promotes overall health and well-being.

There was a time in my life when I refused to pray. I was going through a tough time and felt like prayer wasn't helping. It felt like I was speaking to hear myself talk, and my prayers were being ignored. I initially tried to ignore my feelings of doubt and frustration, and I convinced myself that all I needed to do was pray harder or more frequently. But the more I prayed, the more I became disillusioned.

I eventually stopped praying entirely. I felt that praying was a waste of time and energy and that I should rely on my strength and abilities to overcome difficult times.

When I reflect on that time in my life, I recognize that I was experiencing a crisis of faith. My upbringing with a religious Grandmother instilled in me a belief in the strength of prayer. However, with life's challenges, I wondered if prayer was beneficial. As I matured, I realized that worship is more than just asking for things or seeking divine intervention. It's also about cultivating a sense of connection and gratitude and finding peace and solace in quiet and contemplative moments. In the end, the effectiveness of prayer is a personal and subjective experience that differs for everyone. Whether one has faith in a higher power or not, prayer can offer solace, optimism, and tranquility during periods of anxiety or doubt.

Today, I pray regularly and find that it provides comfort and perspective. I no longer consider prayer a chore or a burden but rather an opportunity to connect with something greater than myself and find meaning and purpose in my life. I hope prayer will do the same for you.

www.ingramcontent.com/pod-product-compliance
Lightning Source LLC
Chambersburg PA
CBHW050324010526
44119CB00003B/98